Who Are You from Home?

Who Are You from Home?

Poems by

Mary Mallek Haines

Cover image by Mary Mallek Haines, "A View of Pierszczewo
village with *tarnina* in bloom"
Cover design by Shay Culligan
Author photo by Fenimore Haines

ISBN: 978-1-63980-487-0

Kelsay Books
502 South 1040 East, A-119
American Fork, Utah 84003
Kelsaybooks.com

Names, like language, anchor us, connect us to family,
home, and nation. When both sets of my grandparents
the Malleks and the Szudareks arrived in America,
they spoke no English. I dedicate these poems to them,
Polish immigrants whose language and customs
thread through my life their indelible design.

"Who Are You from Home?" originated as a second-generation
expression a Polish woman used when asking someone
what her maiden name was. (The saying is still in use
in Wisconsin.) It was viewed in a negative way
by some non-Poles at a time when I was unaware
of ethnic discrimination. In later years, the saying
assumed a quaint, multi-layered meaning—
hence its adoption as the book's title.

Acknowledgments

Thank you to the following publications, in which versions of these poems previously appeared:

Beads of an Abacus: "Ten Sznurek Się Urwie," "A Melody Unheard"

The Poetry Society of Virginia Centennial Anthology: "A Game Board"

The William & Mary Review: "A Game Board"

Contents

Perspective on Flight

A Ghazal

Hustled in the center of a V, a snow goose wrestles in flight;
her wings lose time each time the North wind veers flight.

A Polish woman clings to her infant, the music of home—
a refuge. She questions the motives that trigger flight.

If no oasis appears, your camel runs dry, and day upon day
sands shift in deceit, does salvation deter flight?

"Do I follow my dream?" Joseph asks. "Angels mislead. Maybe
Herod scripted the plot. I dread pursuit, yet cannot counter flight."

Don't ask me where Maryśka comes from. She's a peddler
pocketing stories from a poet, an exile, a dreamer in flight.

Boże Drzewko (God's Little Tree)

They seal the steamer trunk,
shutter the house
they leave as mourners, a home

that shelters a story
they began two years before,
setting providence in motion.

An empty shell, the room
echoes—Helena's first cry,
their nightly whispers.

The voyage will usurp their dreams,
seal Antonie's eyes from Pierszczewo,
her childhood village, its wood cross

rising defiant into the heavens.
Jan will raise another to lift
their New World prayers.

They cannot tarry while *tarnina* buds
burst into spring. And where will they
stow the *Boże drzewko* cutting?

It will drive good roots in America;
its fragrance riding the wind
will spirit their homeland back to them.

What else can they bring from this
they call the Old Country?
What more can a heart carry?

They rise with a chill to the marrow,
trepid hearts racing
toward a land that doesn't speak to them.

Departure, April 1891

Chased by sorrow, they leave Kashubia.
Its soil knows their calloused hands; its fields jealous

for their footfall, horses thundering across the meadow.
Beyond the Atlantic the world falls from the horizon;

the stars obscure. As the ship draws from shore,
their village grows smaller. With each breath

they inhale the journey's bitterness, believe in the sweet.
Will the ocean dismiss them—minnows in a whale's mouth?

A fellow passenger, perhaps a farmer too, stares into
endless tides. He plies the deck in salt-speckled boots—

back and forth, a rhythm that drives them to sleep.
The heart without a compass, stalls.

Antonie hushes Helena with a lullaby, *Lulajże;*
surrounding voices settle like a familiar prayer.

In seven to nine days they will reach America
where they will fall to their knees, like the kings

who traveled from the East, believing in a star.
Soon they will plant the *Boże drzewko* beside the front door.

A Clerk's Lament

The Barge Office, Immigrant Processing Center
New York, 1891

Awash in paperwork, I endure the steamships' surge,
its pour over Manhattan's southeast tip. Each day
I translate illegible faces. Each day 3,000 or more:
Austrian and Polish, Dutch, Slovenian. They begin to look

the same: men in Sunday jackets; wives in bonnets
or babushkas; toddlers fidgeting their mothers' skirts.
Valises, trunks, bundles of weariness. Even a bird in a cage.
How I hate the questions clicking

like a telegraph machine, as I lean my better ear
to accents riffling the air. One syllable trips over another.
A Polish man's name Jan Mallek contradicts
the German ship's manifest: Johann Malek. The man's

bearing straight like a soldier, his manner exact.
I copy the German surname, clip Johann to Joh.
Who can fault me if I err on the side of officialdom?
It's spring. I've more to contemplate than spelling.

A Container

can be a riddle:
it empties when it fills.
It holds and restrains,
opens to the visible or the not-so
like the ocean welcomes a river. A mouth-
ful or half-full, milk gallon,
jelly jar. Jug of wine.
Venom on the tongue. Silence
in an empty house. Germ of a story,
its climax and denouement.
Dying, with its unknowns.
Quirky mind of a poet. Belly of the soul.
Along the tree line, a green porcelain wash tub
spilling ruby begonias. A bird feeder, a bucket,
urns and ossuaries, a cabbage crock, and a closet
with a gold-handle cane, its handle hollow.
Mother's beaver coat; Daddy's mackinaw.
Grandma's beaded Hong Kong evening bag.
A jewelry box with:
a grinning scrimshaw fox,
a Madonna cameo, and a tangle of chains.
No one to explain the rose gold wedding band—
with no initials, no person to claim,
it only withholds.

What's in a Name?

Juliet entreats Romeo to forsake the Montague name:
A rose by any other name will smell as sweet.

"A rose by any other name
will smell as sweet" but overturn
the family garden plot. A rose
called a marigold will sow confusion.

What happens if you drop a letter
        from your name?
What if the gold-handle cane in the closet
(its origin unknown) is hollow after all?

Oh, the stories Daddy wove around Poland.
How his father Jan walked the land
in coattails, as overseer with a cane.
How the Mallek name held an extra "l"

and stood for Polish royalty, enough to crowd
a child's head with castles and pretend.
If a name marries us to home, what of those
who reconfigured theirs to simplify a goal,

or override an intrigue in consonants? Smolinski
shrank to Small. Kostuchowski fell to Kostuch,
and Józef Teodor Konrad Korzeniowski
rose to fame as Joseph Conrad.

Few know the Polish Mikołaj Kopernik, yet hail him
as Copernicus, who threw the world off center.
Science honors Madame Curie but never
utters her Polish name, Maria Skłodowska.

Often lost in marriage, a maiden name remains
rooted to the past. Ask a Polish woman
from our town, "Who are you from home?"
and her answer will pull you into story.

Gramma and the Root Beer Plant

Now I see her plainly:
the prim, planted hat; her brow,
      furrows in a distant field.

A customary lace collar frames
her face, the gaze mournful,
moored to a thought I cannot reach.

Black purse in her right hand,
the other firm around mine, we walk
to Kalpinski Grocers, pausing

at Dad's Old Fashioned Root Beer Plant.
Unlikely pair in the plate glass window.
Bottles march on a conveyor belt:

amber soda into amber glass, a medley—
passage, shadow, and gloss.
Time slows with Gramma beside me,

her language, an ocean between;
Polish phrases swimming
into air. How I want to catch them,

pull them in. I want to know
if Gramma noticed grass poking
between cracks that line the sidewalk

like a map. Home in her chair she waits,
thumbs twirling in her lap,
      a basin filling with worry.

Day Chases Night

between lines and over
the paper's edge where
an ink smudge ends. Cloudy
like rice paper or half-lit scene:

Gramma in her room, closed.
A scent of spearmint candy
        scattered across a plate.
Dryness fills the house,
rooms too dim to remember.

———————————

Night chases day. Shades pulled
in my bedroom awash
in a jaundice tide.

Tangled in fever, I sleep
turning and turning in a womb
that tosses like the sea.

———————————

When mother stepped out
on a windless day,
a salesman rang the bell.
Baring a box
of gleaming blades, he asked
to sharpen our teeth.

My sister recalls
he was selling knives, only selling.

———————————

I believed in my guardian angel
with gold-decked wings and gossamer hair,
creature of flight on a prayer card.

She must have flown to the wrong address
the day a salesman rang the bell,
the day a car with a flashing light
drove Gramma away.

The Quarter in My Pocket

Call it madness. Call it love.
Call it daring when they chose
late November 1930.

On the heels of the Market Crash,
panic throttles the nation. One by one
businesses fail, banks fold.

Dad paraded his new Model A
to St. Casimir Church.
Air bright with wedding bells;

snow like confetti—a quiet, steady
descent on a giddy world.
Dad liked to remind:

"After our wedding all we owned
was a shiny new car
and the quarter in my pocket."

Shantytowns become Hoovervilles;
newspapers, Hoover blankets;
and pockets turned inside out, Hoover flags.

From a silver frame on the wall
the young lovers defy the present
while obeying the photographer's command.

They smile into the future—
Mom wearing loveliness from veil to toe;
Dad notable in white bow tie.

One in four out of work, many hit the road,
traveling from town to city, some by car;
most hitchhike or "ride the rails."

After nuptial blessings, after feast
and dancing, did they forgo *poprawiny,*
the merrymaking of the second day?

Or did they flaunt a fiery polka?
wagering each sigh to satisfy the night
with a promise: "It will never be better."

Between Currents

I.
It snares the wind—a moment, the pelt shivers
       russet against the granary wall. Weathered,
black-rough from years and rain.

The child stands against a backdrop of dahlias profuse
       as her curls. She stares long at the fox, long . . .
expecting it to arch its tail, spring from wall to woods.

Who hung you plush and pretty
       on a rusty peg? Where did you last curl up
in sleep? On a pillow in my picture book?

II.
Mother appears wearing pinafore and braids. Barefoot,
       spindle-legged, she runs through thunder
with a loaf of rye. Remembers gypsies amber-skinned

and wild, who sang and stole in the countryside.
       A child, I strung her stories along
a cotton thread, my stash of winter pearls. Now I swim

between currents at the old farm where the family swing
       stirs—empty. There, between pines,
my cousins chattered, their voices strange.

The Other Side of the Fence

Under a kitchen table with chrome legs,
a little girl sobs. Without a cue,
          the scene moves outdoors.

It's summer. I smell grass,
fresh after mowing.
A moment like this I want
to remember from childhood:
how sunlight falls lustrous

over pasture land where I sit
on my brother's army blanket.
How—feet away—carrots and beans
grow together in cozy rows.

Head in a book, one eye on the cows,
I face my task outnumbered.
I carry my book for company—
and beside me a big stick,
should a bold one charge.

They are dumb animals I'm told,
but I've seen them fighting in the field.
I want to remember them
reaching outrageously long tongues
toward blades of grass
thriving on the other side of the fence.

Epiphany with Swallows

Into the garage they dip,
baby food between their beaks.
So swift, so near air feathers my hair.
A radio blares "to scare
snakes from the nest,"
Lenora shouts over a blues band.

In and out
an open window, barn swallows
flaunt their plumes: indigo, ebony,
sun-flash on the wing.
Below the child looking in.

Back and forth
overhead the birds
rendezvous above the cattle stanchions.
The child on tiptoe strains
toward the rafters, bereft in shadow.

In my dreams a gray cat crouches
on a ledge above a barn window.
A swallow, its fierce wings beating,
flies into its path,
my heart inside the bird.

The House Among Apple Trees

Beyond the clothes line, beyond
a row of spruce,
Daddy built Gramma a house
in our backyard. Ever-so-small,
looking out of place,
it grew among the apple trees.

To the right of its doorstep
stood a fragrant plant. Daddy would snip
a leaf before entering the house,
rub it between his fingers,
breathe in slowly.

On tiptoe one evening my view
through the kitchen window: A blanketed
figure in the back of a gray vehicle,
its flashing red light
twirling, twirling.

Days, weeks, maybe months later,
(What is time to a child?)
a man with red hair drove up
in a big truck and wheeled Gramma's house
away, the house that grew among apple trees.

A patch of sand stared back.
Gone the little house;
gone the fragrant plant.
Silence covered the barren yard,
taking root among the apple trees.

Days, weeks, maybe months later,
relatives I'd never seen gathered
in a roomful of roses
to tell Gramma goodbye.
Whisperings: "she died of a broken heart."

I imagine the house still looking
for the place it once called home.

Ten Sznurek Się Urwie (This String Will Break)

Shunning buttons is easier for Mother.
      Swaddling herself in a fleece jacket,
she settles into her rocking chair

(readies herself unabashedly), rehearsing
      her mother's words:
Ten sznurek się urwie,

as surely as each one finds himself
      cozened in a casket.
Gramma's in blue, prone in a satin exit gown,

rosary beads woven around smooth
      and speckled fingers—
robin eggs within a complex nest.

A necklace floats to the floor unstrung,
      a relic rattles
in a button box—images we carry

      one generation to another.

Waving behind a chain link fence, our daughter
      fragments into diamonds, a pattern
across her face, red shirt, faded jeans. A pattern

pressed while wings of the plane rise, leaving her
      second after second, (pin-point of red) remnant
we are left—and the fragile shell of the heart.

Mother's Emergency Drill

Mother sniffed danger in burnt toast,
heard God's hand in hail, but never spoke
a fearsome word on winter's weather.
A pious woman, she knew the Lord's
omnipotence and drew no shortcuts
when lives were in peril.

At summer thunder's first rumble,
she marched her minions
from the second floor, pillows in tow,
two flights to the basement below.
If a tornado lurked within thirty miles,
she hearkened to tell-tail signs:

yellow streaks in the sky after rain,
the roar of an approaching train.
We probed the skies for color,
strained to hear a doom-spelling sound.

Mother coached in protocol, too:
Under a table or in a closet "crouch
with hands over head," facing proper
direction. Snagged in her worrisome ways,
we often forgot: Was it east or west?
But we never questioned her.

Off the room where drying laundry drooped
in winter, a root cellar's dampness
added terror—we, locked
in the bowels of earth. Nudged between
cellar and sauerkraut crock,
on stormy nights we wavered

between dream and resistance. Father
snoring overhead, never figured in the drill;
we kids too sleepy to question
why he merited an exemption.

Grandma Opachan

Cars rumbling down Highway 51 we raced to name: DeSoto
Studebaker, Pontiac, a game we invented on Bonnie's front steps.

We crossed the highway, crisscrossing back yards,
climbed fences women schemed over, the power

in their aprons. Nightfall fathers traipsed between houses
to a game of canasta commandeered with cigars.

But what did we know? Of the old woman,
who lived in a shoe-like house, not a nursery rhyme;

a woman with no story, no children in sight
until Bonnie and I knocked at her door.

Blind to loneliness, but not to her love
of the Old Country, we pulled from our repertoire

Serdeczna Matko, a hymn that rallied the fire
in her eyes. Center stage we rolled our r's, rounded o's,

pretended Sister Angelica was leading the choir.
Had we pleased enough? Then Grandma pulled from her pocket

the usual shiny nickels. We flew outdoors with our easy-money,
a Polish farewell half-off the tongue.

Her copper skin, rusty knuckles, when she handed us a coin
burned in my mind. The face, crinkled and kind, the kind

that studies you behind a curlicue frame on a museum wall
and follows you to the next room.

A Melody Unheard

It wasn't an official blizzard, only wind
pawing, whining at sills the Christmas Eve
      mother disappeared into the flurries.
      She'd warned: the night someone dies

a dog barks three times. I dreaded closing my eyes.
On the farm three days later, a brood of relatives
circled the wood stove, its kindled sheen lost
      in shadows. Before the camera

Mother and her four sisters perched,
their high heels pecking
the wood floor. Their black skirts
in flight around my face.
      I was five, followed their hands

dabbing their eyes. Their noses red.
Men sat awkward in the parlor
sipping schnapps. Uncle John beside the oilcloth table,
nimble fingers stroking the fiddle strings—
      a melody we'd never heard before.

      Grandma's rickety rocking chair empty
in the corner, while the aunts' voices
stirred with the wind before they grew
distant again, and more
than filled the farmhouse.

The Czar in *Czarnina*

In a Polish household, we celebrated the goose,
saved its down to stuff pillows and the inimitable quilt,
pierzyna, three feet high when fluffed.

The fowl's eventual fate was a pièce de résistance
at holiday tables. Poor goose had no chance to resist.
With ritual hush-hush, a solemn undertone,

its demise remained secret to us younger kids.
I don't recall mention of the act, nor was privy to its staging,
but there was protocol, our brother the oldest reports,

to the ending of a goose. For more than its flesh
was prized. Step one: Dad dealt the executioner's blow—
a blade's swift, clean slit to its scimitar-curved neck.

Mr. Goose, inglorious, hung by his feet from a clothesline,
its blood draining into a basin below. Witness to the victim's
ignominious end? Since he was sole observer,

only big brother can testify. The rest recollect and only agree
on the final step: Mom cooking the goose's vital juice
at the stove where it simmered with allspice, *kubaba,*

named after Kubaba, Hittite goddess of fertility.
How she entered the Polish kitchen, no one knows.
Not many in the family cheered the suspicious creation,

shade of milk chocolate. Mother named it chocolate soup
to tame our imaginations. No one knows, never will,
all the ingredients that lent the dish its velvet texture,

sour-sweet taste, questionable crunch. Our brother said,
"In a pinch duck blood could substitute," but I clearly hear
Mom insisting, "To do it right, only a goose will do."

Our family may quibble on the essence of *czarnina*.
Maybe the word czar in the name signifies its origin in Russia.
Or an exotic, non-Polish land. After all, Kubaba was a Hittite.

The Old Jalopy

The Old Jalopy collapsed
in an empty lot next to Daddy's shop.
The car, ours for the summer—
two girls in pigtails
peering out a haze-swept windshield
beyond the apple orchard,
haystack and barn,

beyond fields aflutter with grasshoppers,
past woods where cows escaped for shade.
Chauffeur and passenger
we sat, smug on the black leather
seats, cotton padding bursting through
the tears. Hands sweaty on the wheel,
you steered out of town fast, far as

Waukesha or Milwaukee, any slick city
where neon signs razzled the night,
where folk in furs and derbies ruled
the street, their hoity-toity talk
and stratagems not unlike those
we hatched on the cracked leather seats.
   We never looked back.

Picking Violets in May

"Look closely among the clover
and timothy grass because
a wild violet is small," Mother says.

It's the Month of Mary,
the month we walk to the pasture
to find violets to set before her statue.

We bend to pick the flowers
hidden in their bed of green.
We pick as quickly as we can,

before they wilt. "Because
they are delicate," Mother says.
Along a rutted path we hurry

home, hurry before the cows,
heavy with milk, head to the barn
along the same path. Their lumbering

bodies rumble the ground when they run,
speeding the thump in my heart.
Back home Mother hums as she

fills the small *kieliszek* with water.
The flowers' skinny stems weave
and sway inside the clear glass.

We place the violets high
on the dresser, where Mary stands—
so high I must step back to see

the purple blossoms,
          leaves the shape of hearts.

Looking In

Invisible as summer yearning
we lazed, leaning
into the shop window—

Maestro Dad at the table saw.
Plank after plank inching
toward its shark teeth.

Wood sheared in crescendo,
tumbling in a sawdust plume,
shavings burying the table legs.

Sunrays through the glass
graced him in a nimbus of light,
an energy none could touch,

nor did he ever look up
        to catch us looking in.

Cock-sure but legally blind in one eye,
Dad kept his saw tuned
through winter's freeze.

He snugged the shop, fed
the potbellied stove long after
the sun sallied over snow drifts.

He poked his head into the cold
on occasion, as if to remind himself
of another world outside.

A Game Board

I.
A father bets heavily on his son;
the mother prone to equal bids.
A thrifty dad, ours shunned money
talk. But how he sang, happy
on whiskey sours:
 I wish I were single,
my pockets would jingle. I wish
I were single again.

II.
In Antonia Fortress Roman soldiers
engraved a game board in stone—
each move a reminder.
They rolled dice
for the Rebel's crimson cloak.

III.
A mother divided herself among
her children, but like an orange
shared, not always equal
the division, not always sweet
an investment. She has yet to retrieve
her thought, her vision.

IV.
That each of us dies
for love is poetry enough.

V.
The Father wagered on the son's fall.
Surely he knew where the mother would
stand, looking up at broken flesh.
Tears kissed the ground
and the earth closed, before it opened.

Nature's Hold

I came to the water's edge to say goodbye:
      soon you'll be gone—your distant eyes
tell me. Here, far from the familiar, trees stand

lush, twinned in the lake. Higher up the mountain,
      they appear blue. Parting's not a color we wear well.
Light changes everything: reflections skim the water at dusk,

more real than evergreens on sturdy feet.
      An almost-spent sun nudges the sky into night,
changes the shadows moving across the lake.

Ripples grow in ever widening circles far from shore.
      But missing you breaks nature's hold—I long to reach
the other side knowing, nothing, even loss, is lost.

The Virgin in the Room

In the forbidden room on the north side of the house,
(like *Alice in Wonderland* when the clock stopped),

I knelt at my perch on a window bench.
Outdoors a swath of finch huddled.

Thistle plants drew them, plush gold feathering
a raft in a river of grass. No one would find

me here in Mom and Daddy's room,
door closed, bed covered in chenille spread

blue and white like a sky rolled-out. Across
a doily, Daddy's spare change scattered. Everything else

in place. A Blessed Virgin on the armoire beckoned,
forlorn in blue robe, plaster of Paris chipped.

How worn the blush on her cheek.
How drab the white veil, the hands pointing to

her heart that a dagger divides in two. "Your own heart
a sword shall pierce," Simeon warned.   One day

I'd paint the statue's robe, every bruise, every fold.
Paint it blue like new again, but nothing to alter the heart.

A Tall Man

For my father

To me you were a tall man
who walked among the trees—
a straight, unswerving line
against a steel-blue sky.
       To you I was Maryśka.

A summer afternoon after church,
we circled the fairground racetrack,
the two of us
       in a crowd.

Sulky wheels and horses
churned the course to clouds,
the beating hooves and my heart
racing and the crowd for an instant
       held its breath.

Wherever we walked
       (your stride crisp and measured),
I stretched to keep in step. You'd stop,
always stop to banter with friends;

your arms like a bellow moving
       your words in and out.
I had no need to talk,
just be there, Maryśka, to hold your hand;
and all the world
       fell in place.

Rosemary in Sorrow

There's rosemary, that's for remembrance.

Like Ophelia I riddle in rhyme.
My words to you Father lie
sealed inside a casket of lead.
Over time it weighs
like loss whose lid is lightest
       when unopened.

In my garden rosemary stands
cold against January snow.
Its fragrant needles slipped
between the hands of the dead
cannot conceal decay. Even
sorrow masks as madness.

Who played the ruse more
than Hamlet, his words tipped
in poison? He left Ophelia
fatherless as I, without defense.
If rosemary brings remembrance,
save it for spring.

I slipped the letter beneath your lapel
as you lay, Father, hands folded.
You closed your eyes while I
cooked dinner a thousand miles away.
There's rosemary, fennel, and rue
       enough to share.

Ascension

Along North Second Street she walks
to church; as usual, Romie her man
on the opposite side. The hat he wears
sags, as if left in a rain that stole its shape.

Romie shouts over the rush and rumble
of cars, his response a contretemps to Angie.
Some days his voice tapers,
hymn to her antiphon: back and forth,
two spirits crossing in flight.

At Mass one Sunday morning, Romie springs
from the pew onto his seat, hat in hand,
waving toward the vaulted ceiling.
The curious turn from the altar,

eyes on the hat fanning the air—up, up
to a sparrow circling in frenzy, diving over
our heads. Angie on her knees;
Romie, a mimicry of flight, totters at the edge.

On his face a broad-rimmed smile, wide and wider,
as if he too might rise and enter the Heavenly Hosts.

"It's almost spring,"

        we sing in uncertainty,
each March sun stipples
its design on snow.
For months a county plow muscles

down roads, through drifts.
Truck wheels sully, and slush
overwhelms until snow succumbs:

flakes turn to crystal, ground's cover
trickles to rivulet, to river, to the sea
we've never seen.

        Then what surprise
to waken to a plow's grumble,
its push and lumber, and track its light
ghost across the bedroom wall.

I raise the shade and merge
into night swimming
in snow, its down, its shimmer—
        silent seduction

so boundless the mind's compass
can never circle 'round,
nor soul share.

        No doubt heaven's awake;
it spills its trove flake
by flake, while the house sleeps on
to the familiar furnace wheeze.
Am I the only one to hear?

Photo Ritual

They spill from a shoebox,
a shuffle of time at the kitchen table.
Like a card player, I draw
from a pool of memories.

Tomboy in bangs, barefoot
in a flour sack dress, you hug
a scraggly kitten, next to
brother Alex clutching a rooster.

1929 scrawled on the back of this one:
Daddy courting you, sweet seventeen,
on the running board of his Model A.
Claims he drove ninety miles one way
to hold your hand in Sunday's parlor.

Who's the woman with moon-drawn
eyes, lithe arms in a flapper dress?
You—always in a housecoat, bib apron,
graying waves held back by a hairnet.

Are you the woman who carried
a gunny sack with Sunday's dinner hen
on its way to a chopping block?
The woman who photographed cows,
        called them by name?

Here's one of Daddy wreathed with trees
beside a ragged space—for years a mystery.
One of us kids mistook you for a stranger
and tore you from the photo,
        tore you from his side.

Beyond Day's End

Through half-drawn draperies—
Mother in a rocking chair huddles
with the book. Evening will find her,

silent lips still moving adagio
to moon's glow shifting
past her shoulder, onto a page.

Bóg Mój i Wszystko, My God and All,
gold letters on the leather spine—
her prayer book, quiet link to faith.

When I was a child, Mother folded
my hands in prayer. I'd close my eyes
to night opening a friendlier face:

monsters under the bed swimming
off to a watery cage,
the room filled with her voice.

Kneeling in the dark,
we recited the *Ojcze Nasz,* "Our Father,"
threshold to a place beyond day's end.

I memorized each foreign word, each
tangle of consonants, ignorant of import,
aware of embrace.

The volume's edges pale now;
on empty days I fan through its pages,
pause at its demands on my tongue.

Long enough to hear Mother's voice,
to hold the light
        drifting over her shoulder.

Ode to the Polish Blues

Powder-face. Cavalier sneak.
Mood swinger. Why deceive
with carnelian sunsets, lavender
love letters, moonful eyes?
Stalker of poets, balladeers,
you embrace like Judas.

I'll harangue you, chap,
turn you inside out. In spite,
I'll brandish sniffles
in public, applaud mourning
doves, relish *Romeo and Juliet*
for its pathos, graffiti subway walls

with "I Love Melancholia." Yet—
without you, Gershwin's "Blue Monday
Blues" might have been "The Reds,"
Ophelia's madness a baffling matter,
and Chopin's "Nocturne in E flat major"
just another polka.

About the Author

Mary Mallek Haines, a writer of Polish ancestry and author of the poetry collection *Beads of an Abacus* (San Francisco Bay Press, 2011), was raised in Stevens Point, Wisconsin. She has an M.A. in English from the University of South Florida, where she taught as an adjunct. As a military wife she lived in Germany and in Japan, as well as several U.S. states, before settling in Williamsburg, Virginia, with her husband Charles. Since then, she has devoted much of her time to poetry related activities. For five years she hosted monthly poetry readings at a local coffeehouse, and she served as vice-president of the eastern region of the Poetry Society of Virginia. She also initiated a poetry class, "Poetry: Writing Your Story," for female inmates at the county jail. As a Virginia Master Naturalist, her favorite interests are observing and photographing birds, butterflies, and nature's endless surprises.